Raymond Loewy Foundation for the Promotion of Contemporary
Industrial Design

Visions of Design
edited by Uta Brandes

Now is the Perspective

>Vieni, date me la benedizione.«
W. A. Mozart

Karl Lagerfeld, third winner of the Lucky Strike Designer Award ■■
Bases have the unfortunate habit of debasing monuments — for they
merely rob us of the last vestige of mental mobility, real or imagined,
and thereby destroy the very act of thinking. ■ On the other hand: people are evidently in great need of stopping places in order to find the
serenity of insight, to grasp their thoughts, to follow new paths. A link
between rest and movement, between continuum and event is of the
essence — and leads to those curiously bumpy paths that we are forever
stumbling along, oblivious to categorial or exemplary understanding.
We just keep going, no questions asked. ■ But design may well offer a
few ideas that could foster understanding, for it is a discipline that
functions squarely between these two poles: between music that is
fleeting (which probably makes it so moving) and architecture that is
static (which possibly makes it so depressing). This in turn accounts for
the Lucky Strike Designer Award: it represents an attempt to halt the
social and disciplinary dynamic for a fleeting moment, to highlight the
work of a designer, so as to inspire reflection on past experience and
open up the possibility of pursuing new directions. ■ This has been and
will continue to be documented, enhanced, and expanded in a monograph on the winner of the Lucky Strike Designer Award, a book of work
in progress as a dynamic interface between historical presentation and
the future it constructs or deconstructs. However, this year in 1993 a
monograph will not be published because the institution Karl Lagerfeld
is not compatible with this kind of open-ended approach. Understand-
ably so, because his »now« is always the season to come, his present is
always history, and his backward look consistently becomes a vanish-
ing point in which the ruins of history are refined into the tools of his
trade. ■ No wonder then that this link in the series has become a photo
essay, since Lagerfeld's handle on history is virtually an immanent
description of the photographic universe, one that should actually be
called »melanographic« (with the blessings of Mallarmé, Raoul Haus-
mann, and John Cage). ■ The jury chose to give the Lucky Strike
Designer Award to Karl Lagerfeld for his exceptional mastery of design
management, for his precise demonstration of the complexity of design
and the economic success of design thus implemented, and for his engi-
neering of daily culture. The jury did so, knowing full well that today not
only history but also design management, financial success, and daily
culture are inevitably, incorrigibly bound up with stories. Because only
stories can project the now into the future.

Michael Erlhoff
President of the Board of Trustees of
the Raymond Loewy Foundation

KARL LAGERFELD
off the record

SCALO

Karl Lagerfeld — off the record | Editors: Gerhard Steidl, Walter Keller ■ Design: Hans Werner Holzwarth, Design pur, Berlin, in cooperation with Gerhard Steidl and Walter Keller | Production: Gerhard Steidl, Bernard Fischer ■ Typography, Lithos, Printing: Steidl, Göttingen ■ © Karl Lagerfeld 1994 | © 1994 Steidl Verlag, Göttingen ■ Licensed edition for Scalo Publishers, Zurich— Berlin—New York, with the kind permission of Steidl Verlag, Göttingen ■ © for this edition: Scalo Publishers, Weinbergstrasse 22 a, 8001 Zurich, Switzerland | Tel. 41/1/261-0910, Fax 41/1/261-9262. USA: c/o D.A.P., 636 Broadway, New York, N.Y., 10012, Tel. 212 473 5119, Fax 212 673 28 87 ■ All rights reserved. No photograph of Karl Lagerfeld and no part of this book may be reproduced in any form whatsoever without prior written permission from the publisher, in particular the use of any part hereof in newspapers or magazines, in public speeches, in films or dramatizations, on radio or on television. This includes single pictures or passages. Exceptions are made for pictures in direct association with reviews of this book. The publisher is happy to answer inquiries. ■ First edition April 1995 ■ ISBN 1-881616-37-1

This book is dedicated to Eric Pfrunder,

without whom it could never have happened.

1952–1955 14, Rue de la Sorbonne

I lived in the Gerson Hotel, 14, Rue de la Sorbonne from 1952 to 1955. M. and Mme Zapusec ran a "boarding house" for minors and students, with great empathy, with warmheartedness and a great understanding of budding freedom. It was like the film "Sous le Ciel de Paris". I had two rooms and a balcony on the fifth floor. At the time, I felt the world was mine or would be soon.

1955–1957 32, Rue de Varenne

The only modern building on this famous 18th-century street.
Bad luck! Housing was scarce in Paris in the fifties. It was
built in the thirties and had a marvellous view of Paris with the
Eiffel Tower, Sacré-Cœur, and the Arc de Triomphe. It was a
duplex apartment and the landlady, a former haute-couture
saleswoman, kept a closer watch on me than Mme Zapusec in
the Rue de la Sorbonne.

1957 31, Rue de Tournon

My own apartment at last and an 18th-century building!
Nobody keeping an eye on me anymore. I could finally do what
I wanted! Unfortunately the dream only lasted one year. But I
still love that street.

1958—1959 19, Rue Jacob

You had to go through the courtyard to reach this apartment. It used to be a ballroom, and the view overlooking the park with Delacroix's studio was very poetic. A typical Parisian surprise.

1959–1963 7, Quai Voltaire

The most beautiful view in the world (for me, at the time) of
the Seine and the Louvre. My neighbor on the first floor was
the Marquis de Cuevas.
You could never open the windows in summer — the noise of
the traffic was deafening even in those days.

1963–1973 35, Rue de l'Université

Here I spent ten of the most carefree and happiest years of
my life. I was advised to leave the building — because the
apartment would bring bad luck. Everyone who moved in after
I left died in some mysterious way.

1974–1977 6, Place St. Sulpice

Everything was perfect here except that I didn't like the
building and had the feeling it was bringing me bad luck.
I tried to get back to the 7th arrondissement as fast as
possible. Seven is my lucky number.

1977... 51, Rue de l'Université

until my departure for Monte Carlo

The most beautiful doorway on the Rue de l'Université
(designed in 1788 by Ledoux). I love these great mysterious
"portes cochères". They are like guardians of mystery. The
great novels of French literature and countless scenes in
French history take place behind doors like that.

Axel

Patricia Boissiere Arnal

Helen Bonhan-Carter

Pascal Brault

Naomi Campbell

Héléna Christensen

Frédéric David

Donaes

Linda Evangelista

Polly Hamilton

Shalom Harlow

Eva Herzigova

Yannick d'Is

Philippe Kerboriou

Lisa Lovatt Smith

Stéphane Marais

Kristen McMenamy

Wallis Montana

Heidi Morawetz

Franciane Moreau

Moti

Zazie de Paris

Oribe

Brandi Quinones

Nick Rodgers

Gilles Rollet

Olivier Saillant

Eve Salvail

Sasha

Claudia Schiffer

Paméla Sneed

Bernward Sollich

André Léon Talley

Anna Thalbach

Katharina Thalbach

Emma Thompson

Claus Tober

Christy Turlington

Patricia Velasquez

Virginie Viard

Toni Ward

Christian Williams

Eric Wright

Julien d'Ys

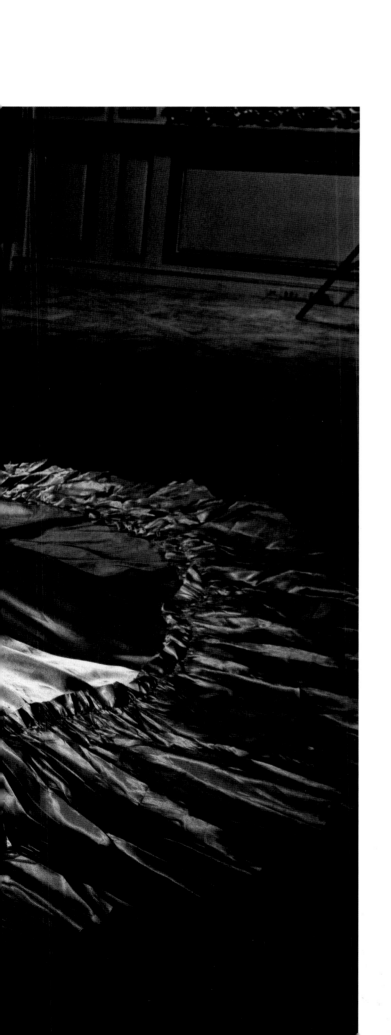

ILE DE FRANCE

the forgotten

chapel

HOMMAGE À MARY WIGMAN

for Emma Thompson

Paris 7ème

Entre Cour et Jardin, as they say in France.
Façades hint at the magic of noble courtyards,
hidden from the public eye.

St. Cloud Park, April 1994

This is where the famous Princess Palatine lived.

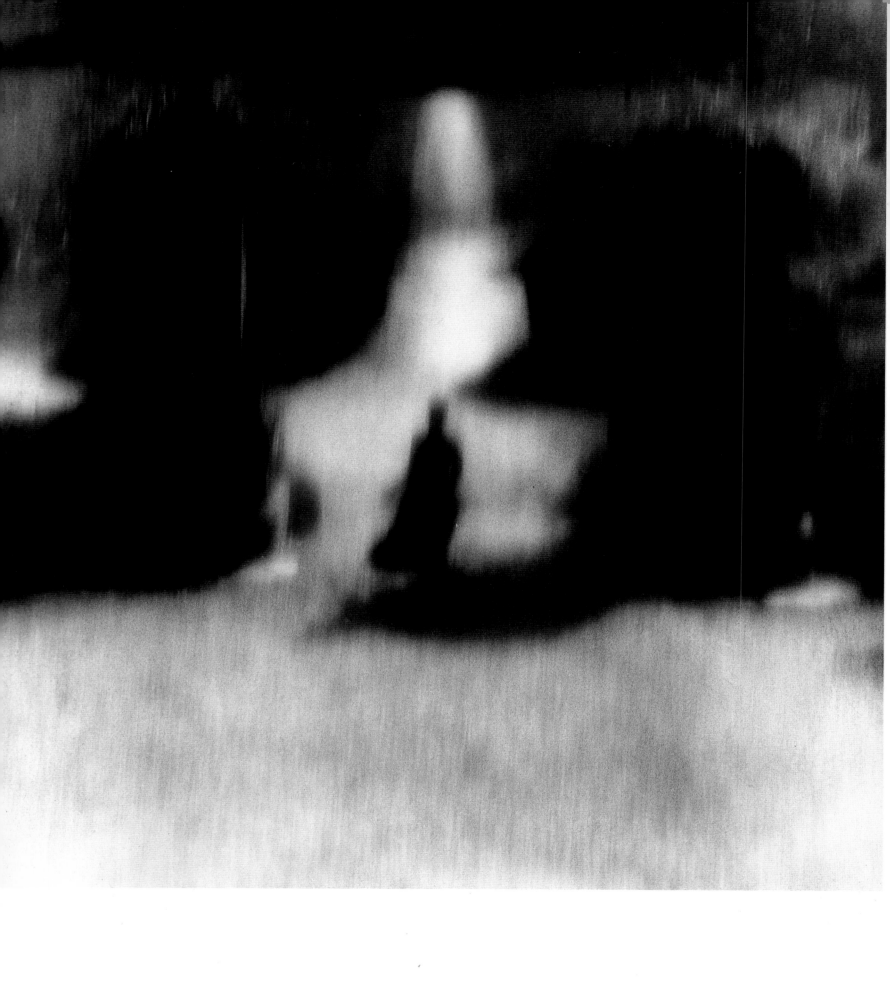

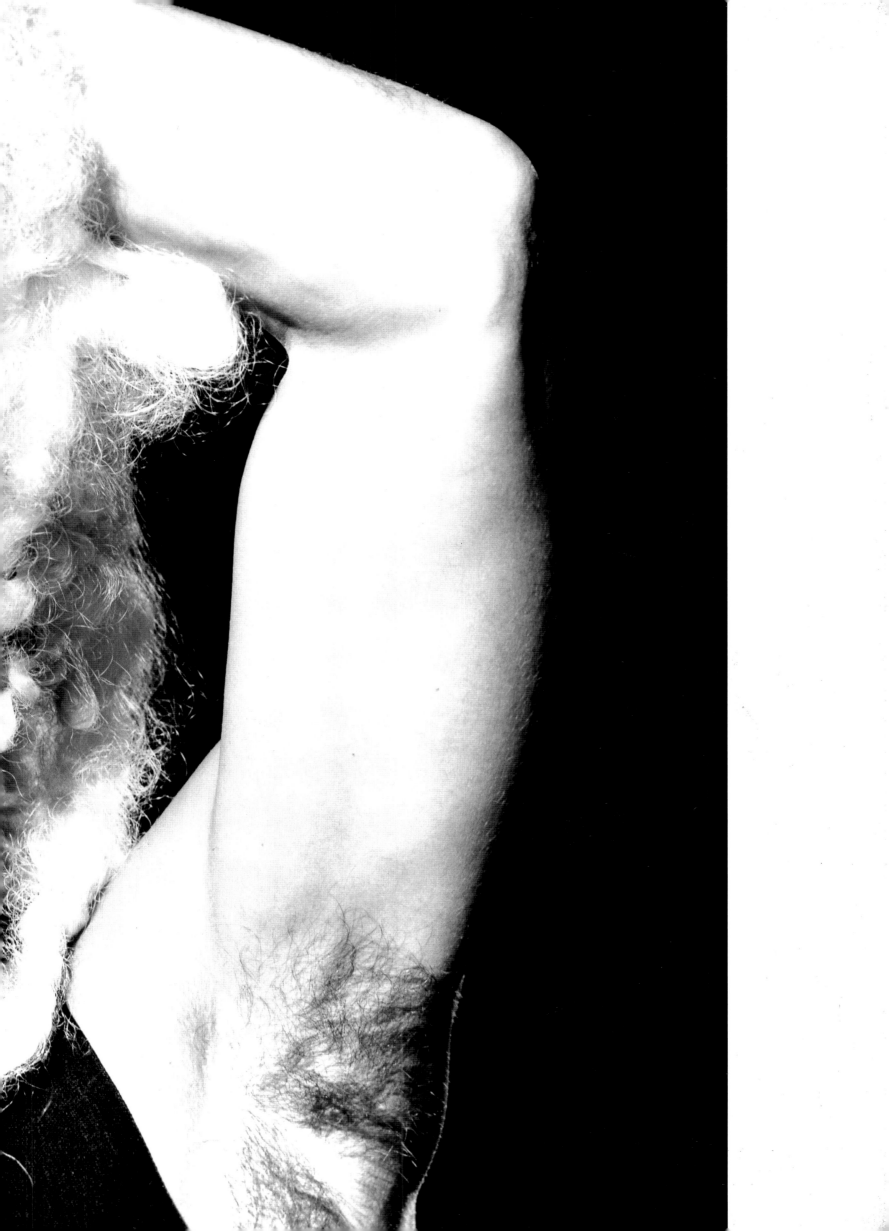

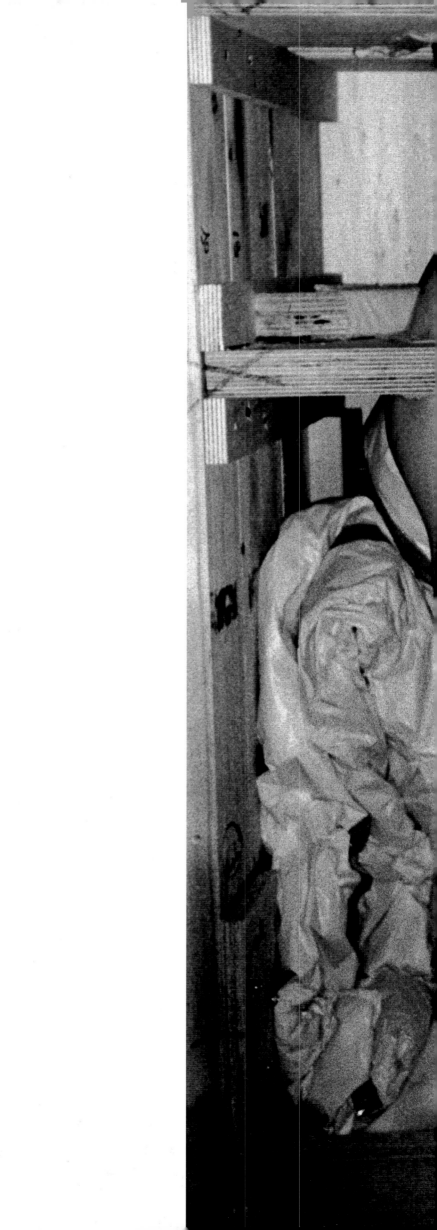

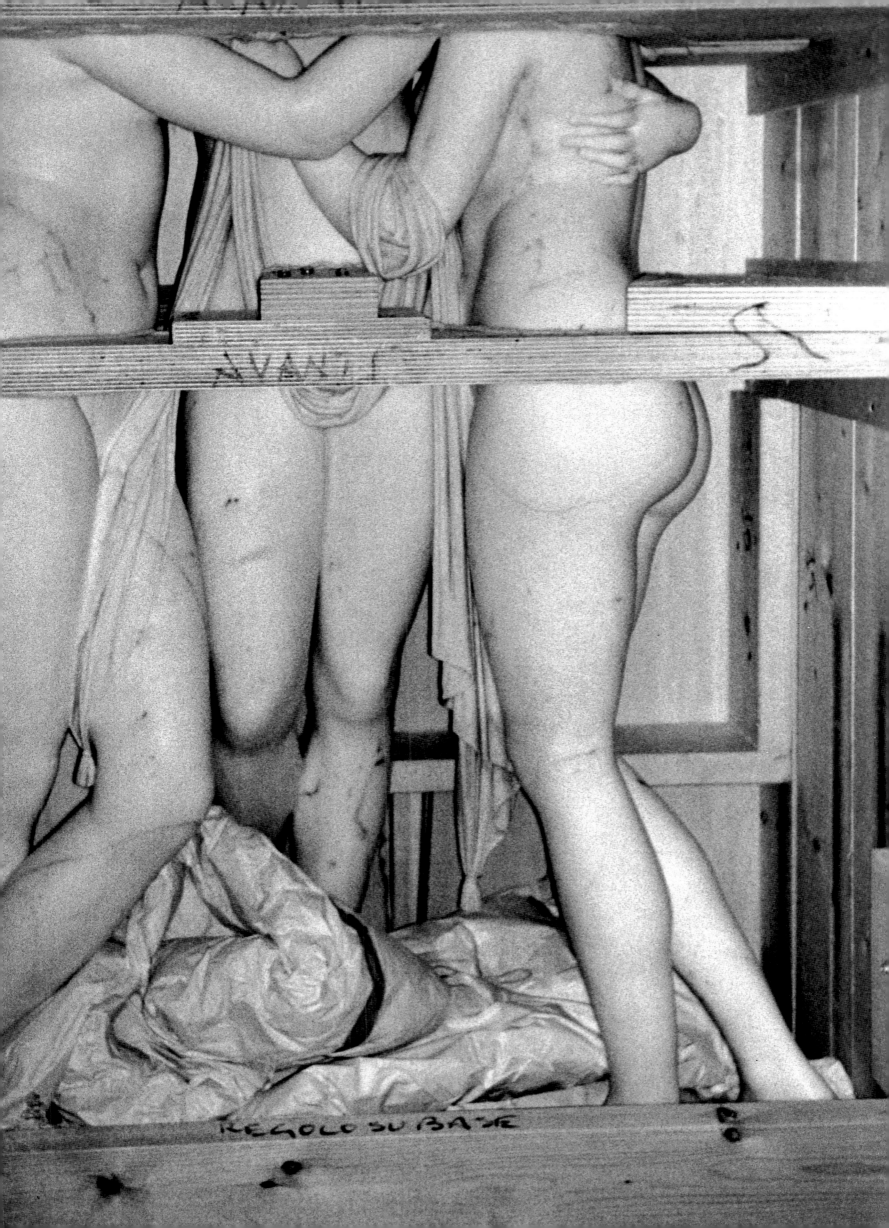

Château de Roussan

Linda in the Castle of Roussan

Linda Evangelista in
THE WALK IN

THE SNOW

AFTERNOON OF A

FAUN

Variations on a Theme by Mallarmé

Claudia Schiffer starring in

NIX

(which in Berlin's dialect means "nothing")
or the simple, naive and moral story of
Greta's and Hans' trip to Berlin

A Heimat Film

They are students and have very little money...

Hans and Greta stay in her strange great-uncle's little apartment in former East Berlin. The building and the courtyard are very neglected as are many houses in that part of Berlin. Greta's uncle is away. He was an officer in the last war and was never married. The small apartment is very stuffy, cosy and very "German". Greta's uncle has lots of knick-knacks and souvenirs.

P.S. You can believe me or not, everything was like that in this apartment. I did not move one piece ... It's unbelievable but true.

To make a little money they go to the flea market, named "Zille-Markt" in Berlin, and Greta sells a ring to Mme Boettcher. This lady has two friends who have a very good contact to the "scene" as they call the underground world of Berlin. One is Medi, who falls in love with Greta and Klaus, a bad boy and barman. Officially Medi, the Turkish boy, works at the flea market. But could he be Madame Boettcher's lover?

Klaus works as a barman in a club which belongs to Madame Francine, a Frenchwoman, who is the former wife of a German called Falkenberg. Francine is also a good friend of Medi's. Klaus and Medi take Greta and Hans to the club which is open until very late at night . . .

... and where transvestites meet; one of them used to work as a babysitter in the late
afternoon.
Hans is unhappy seeing Greta flirting with Medi.

The star in Madame Francine's Late Night Show is a French transvestite called "Cri-Cri de Paris". Madame Francine and Medi urge Greta to sing and dance as well. She likes the idea . . .

Nevertheless Greta tries to continue her studies.

But her thoughts are elsewhere ...

One afternoon, Greta is alone in her uncle's apartment.

Medi comes to see her ...

In a closet they find a helmet which belonged to the father of Greta's uncle. They play strange games.

Greta is naive but also a bit depraved, more than she ever thought she could be.

In a way this photo tells us everything about our story. It is almost a symbol for Germany and all its problems — both of yesterday and today.

Madame Francine also has a shop which sells beautiful clothes. Greta is mad about them.

But how to pay for all of them? Madame Francine knows a way out ... (like Valeska Gert in "Die freudlose Gasse" with Greta Garbo).

Madame Francine is mad for Medi.

Madame Francine's milliner brings a beautiful hat to the shop ...
The hat in his hand is the one Greta is wearing.

Greta is becoming the star in Madame Francine's notorious club ...

She is beautifully dressed.

Madame Boettcher goes there as well, with her former partner, Hotte Reichlich.

Medi, too, is getting more sophisticated.

He finds this strange doll in a locked closet in the apartment of Greta's uncle.

Medi's affair with Greta continues. But her mind is somewhere else. She is dreaming of a more sophisticated life, of luxury etc. ... and of another kind of man.

Greta is becoming very sophisticated. She only goes back to the apartment to visit poor Hans, who continues his studies and is very unhappy.

One night, before she goes out, she comes to see him to tell him that everything is over.
She is cruel and tender at the same time ...

The unhappy Hans stays behind alone...

"Life means 'defend yourself'" is written over his bed.

Greta is now the woman in Berlin. She is now known as "Gritta". She lives in a chic hotel and leads a superficial life of fake luxury. She gives Medi lessons of savoir vivre. She and Medi are sometimes still lovers.

One night Hans comes to see her. She understands that everything she has been seeking has nothing to do with real life ...
They decide to leave Berlin, all they experienced was a single "NIX" (NOTHING).

They move out of the little apartment and start a new life.

Greta is now a very different woman from the young student with braids who came to Berlin. She is now a woman who has learnt about life and made her choices.

THE DUCHESS OF WINDSOR

admire people who are not great beauties but who become icons of elegance by willpower alone. In my memory there is no rival to the Duchess of Windsor. She acquired taste the way others buy antiques. ■ Her best years started at an age when women of her generation thought it was already too late. She fascinated the Duke for the rest of his life. ■ Crossing and uncrossing her skinny legs on a gilded front-row seat in a couture salon was her most important occupation. ■ I have the feeling that she never really liked fashion, that she loved clothes only to show her silhouette. She never wanted to be sexy, but in those days ambitions were different, and she was the most ambitious one of them all. ■ Her style and looks were part of the couture and grooming of another era. Hers were modern looks with old standards that now appear rigorously Spartan. Ruffles were not invented for her. ■ Her approach to fashion was a kind of connoisseurship. She could never be a real fashion influence like Garbo or Hepburn. Her elegance in its final form was a bore: a fashion queen who never really entered the throne room of fashion. ■ For these photographs I included the latest silhouette I designed for Chanel, because the Duchess loved to be first with the new. ■ I liked her best in Schiaparelli and some Mainbocher. To be honest, I think her pale-blue Mainbocher wedding dress was unbecoming. (Her narrow, boyish hips pulled it off.) A Schiaparelli suit gave her a military harshness, the word best describing her style and her attitude. Dior of the 50's was unbecoming for a woman of her generation, except for a few evening dresses. ■ She was never beautiful, but she could create a kind of beauty without the slightest shadow of visible doubt. Her vanity was an art form. Looking at her photos, you see that her mask was a thin one. Good bones and a big head gave her personality. She never looked young, but there was never a soft or chubby touch of middle age either. ■ Her hairdo ended up looking like the wig of an old Chinese empress. (She had lived in the Far East, after all.) ■ There was really no gender about her. She looked a little mannish in all her couture dresses. But in the end she appealed neither to men nor to women but to high fashion alone. ■ We will never know what she really felt or thought. We can only rely on her face, her clothes and her jewelry. No real memoirs of any interest, no intimate confessions survive, just superficial interviews, and a lot of truth — and gossip.

Bassin Deligny, June 1992

Royalton Hotel, November 1993

LES LIAISONS

DANGEREUSES